# THE MORTGAGE MINDSET

## A MORTGAGE BOOK THAT SPEAKS HUMAN™

## LILY DOMINGUEZ

LILY D PUBLISHING

**LILY D PUBLISHING**

ISBN (Hardcover): 979-8-9940670-1-7

ISBN (Ebook): 979-8-9940670-2-4

**Cover Design:** Lily D Publishing

**Interior Design:** Lily D Publishing

*To my sons, Andresito and Alejandro — loves of my life, my greatest joy, my purpose, and the reason behind everything I do. You are my heart walking outside my body, the reminder that every challenge is worth it, and every victory sweeter when shared with you.*

*To Michel, who reminds me every single day that I have what it takes to succeed — that I'm ready, capable, and built for greatness. Your constant encouragement has been the quiet strength behind every page.*

*To my mother, the first writer in our family — thank you for passing down your love for words and creativity.*

*And to my dear friends, clients, and colleagues— thank you for sharing your stories, your trust, and your dreams.*

*You've each left fingerprints on these pages and inspired the lessons within them.*

# CONTENTS

# NOTE FROM THE AUTHOR

If you're holding this book, you're probably thinking about buying a home… or you already did and you're wondering, "What the heck just happened?"

Either way, you're in the right place.

My clients always tell me the same thing:

*"Why doesn't anyone explain this stuff in normal words?"*

So I decided to fix that.

I wrote this book the same way I talk to my clients — with honesty, warmth, a little humor, and zero judgment. Because the truth is, buying a home isn't just about interest rates and paperwork. It's about emotions. Stability. Dreams. Stress. Excitement. Fear. And yes, money.

This book is a safe space to learn, to laugh, and to finally understand the mortgage world without feeling lost or embarrassed. You're not supposed to already know this stuff. That's why I'm here.

Grab a coffee. Get comfy. We're doing this together. 🩶

— Lily

\* \* \*

# ☕ PREFACE

## THE HEART BEHIND THE MORTGAGE MINDSET

Let me tell you a secret: most people don't buy a home — they just *survive* the process.

They walk into the mortgage process with confidence, and somewhere between "Send me your documents" and "Congratulations, you're clear to close," they lose all sense of calm, control, and clarity. And honestly? It's not their fault.

The mortgage world can feel like a maze built by people who assume you already know the rules.

I wrote this book because I've seen clients break down in tears from confusion… and then light up with relief once things were finally explained in plain English. I've seen people make brilliant financial decisions — and others get trapped simply because no one took the time to educate them.

You deserve better.

You deserve a guide that talks to you like a real human being, not a spreadsheet.

You deserve to understand the "why," not just the "what."

And you deserve a home buying experience that feels empowered, not pressured.

To make this journey simple, I guide you using something I call *The Speaks Human System*™ — a communication approach I created to break complex mortgage concepts into clear, empathetic, human language. You'll see this approach throughout the book, woven gently into every explanation and example.

My goal isn't just to teach you mortgages — it's to shift your entire mindset around money, homeownership, and long-term wealth. When you understand how this world really works, you make better decisions. You walk into the process like someone who knows exactly what they're doing.

And you will.

By the last chapter, you'll have a confidence most people never get. And you'll have earned every bit of it.

* * *

# HOW TO USE THIS BOOK

This book is designed to be read however *you* need it:

### ☞ If you're just starting:

Begin at Chapter 1. The mindset foundation will make everything else so much easier.

### ☞ If you already know you're buying soon:

Skip to the chapters that talk about pre-approval, shopping, offers, and closing.

### ☞ If you want to build or protect wealth:

Head to Chapter 11. That's where the big-picture strategy lives.

### ☞ If you're overwhelmed:

Read one chapter at a time. Each one is short, clear, and meant to reduce stress, not add to it.

☞ **If you have a highlighter:**

Use it. A lot.

☞ **If you're reading this with a glass of wine...**

Honestly? That's the best way.

Most importantly:

This book is not homework.

It's your guide, your coach, and your "finally someone explains this!" companion.

Read it straight through, jump around, or revisit chapters as life changes — you'll understand the mortgage world more clearly every time.

* * *

# ⭐ CHAPTER 1

## MINDSET MATTERS: THE REAL START OF THE HOME BUYING JOURNEY

Let's start with something nobody tells you:

Buying a home is not just a financial decision — it's an emotional one.

And if your mindset isn't right, even the strongest pre-approval won't save you from the stress spiral.

You know exactly what I'm talking about.

One minute you're excited, scrolling through listings and dreaming about kitchen islands...

and the next minute you're on Google at 2 a.m. searching:

*"Can you buy a house if you ate ramen for dinner three nights in a row?"*

Listen.

We're not doing that.

This chapter is all about getting your mind into the right place so the rest of the journey feels doable — even enjoyable.

Because here's the real deal:

A calm, confident buyer makes better decisions, handles surprises like a champ, and actually remembers to breathe during the process.

## Why Mindset Matters

I've helped hundreds of buyers, and here's the pattern I see every single time:
A buyer who believes they can do this… does it.
A buyer who feels terrified, ashamed of their finances, or "not ready enough"… gets stuck.
You don't need perfect credit.
You don't need a giant savings account.
You don't need to have your entire life figured out.
You just need a clear mindset and a willingness to learn.
That's what this book is — not a lecture, not a math exam, not a bunch of confusing lender jargon.
This is your calm, confident, "talk to me like I'm human" guide.

## The Fear That Nobody Talks About

If we're keeping it real:
Money is emotional.
It brings up childhood memories, old habits, and that little voice in your head that says:
*"Are you sure you're ready for this?"*
And sometimes that voice is loud. Sometimes it's right.
Sometimes it's just dramatic. But once you understand how this process works — like, actually works — fear shrinks.

Confidence grows.
Information becomes power instead of panic.
As we move through the chapters, I'll keep using this same Speaks Human approach so everything feels clear and stress-free.

## The Mindset Shift

Here's the shift we're making:

**From:** "I don't know anything about mortgages."
**To:** "I know enough to make smart decisions."

**From:** "I'm probably going to make a mistake."
**To:** "I'm prepared, supported, and capable."

**From:** "This is overwhelming."
**To:** "I can do this — one step at a time."

And I'm walking with you through every single one.

## What You'll Get From This Chapter (and This Book)

By the time we're done, you'll be:
• more confident
• more informed
• more prepared
• and way less stressed

You'll understand the mortgage world in a way that feels normal — not like someone is reading IRS tax code to you. You'll get clarity. You'll get peace of mind. And you'll get tools that help you make decisions based on facts, not fear. Because the truth is, you don't just need information — you need a mindset that supports your goals.

And that mindset starts here.

\* \* \*

# ⭐ CHAPTER 2

## READY, SET, BUY! (GETTING YOURSELF TRULY READY)

Let's talk about "**readiness.**"

Most people think being ready to buy a home means having perfect credit, zero debt, and $50,000 sitting in a savings account like a decorative plant.

Reality check?

Almost nobody buying their first home looks like that.

Being *ready* isn't about perfection — it's about understanding your situation and knowing what steps to take next.

You don't need a flawless financial résumé. You just need clarity.

### Step 1: Know Your "Why"

Before you scroll Zillow until your thumb hurts, ask yourself:

• Why do I actually want to buy?

• What problem am I trying to solve?

• What would a new home give me that I don't have now?

Maybe you need more space. Maybe your rent just went up *again*. Maybe you're tired of hearing your upstairs neighbor vacuum at 11 p.m.

Your "why" keeps you grounded when the emotions hit — and trust me, they will.

## Step 2: Know Your Numbers (Gently)

This isn't the moment to panic or judge yourself.

You simply need to know:

• How much you earn

• Your monthly obligations

• Your debt

• Your comfort level

• A realistic down payment

No shame. No stress. Just facts.

## Step 3: Start Gathering Your Docs

Buying a home requires paperwork. A lot of paperwork. Think of it like gathering ingredients before cooking. Once you have everything in place, the recipe (your mortgage!) comes out beautifully.

## Step 4: Build Your Team

You shouldn't be doing this alone. Get a lender you trust (hi ), a realtor who listens, and support from people who want to see you succeed — not scare you.

## Step 5: Prepare Emotionally

Buying a home is exciting… and it also comes with: doubts, fears, and a lot of Google searches.

But with the right mindset and guidance, you'll navigate this with a lot more confidence than you expect.

* * *

## THE SPEAKS HUMAN SYSTEM™

### Clarity • Empathy • Confidence

**Clarity:** so you understand what's happening, without jargon.

**Empathy:** because money is emotional and mortgages are stressful.

**Confidence:** so you make strong, informed decisions at every step.

*A simple approach to make the mortgage world feel human.*

# ★ CHAPTER 3

## CREDIT CONFIDENCE: UNDERSTANDING YOUR SCORE WITHOUT THE STRESS

Let's break this down without stress:

Your credit score is NOT a moral evaluation. You are not a "good" or "bad" person based on a number. You're human. And humans borrow money, pay bills late sometimes, and forget subscriptions exist. It's okay.

### ★ What Lenders Look For

A lender looks at your score the same way a landlord looks at references — not to judge you, but to understand how you manage money.

Here's what really matters:

• Payment history

• Credit card usage

- Length of credit

- Types of credit

- New accounts

No puzzles. No gatekeeping. Just criteria.

## The Magic of Credit Utilization

This one rule alone can bump your score:

Use less than 30% of your credit limits.

Under 10%? Chef's kiss.

Even a tiny over-the-limit charge can drop your score more than you expect — not because you're irresponsible, but because the algorithm is... dramatic.

## Collections & Mistakes

If you've had collections, late payments, or "oops" moments? You're normal.

Most buyers have something in their history. Your job now is to understand your report and make a plan.

## Building Confidence

Credit is not about perfection. It's about direction.

If you're improving — even slowly — that's already progress. And lenders *love* progress.

My clients always worry about their credit. Then we review it together, create a plan, and suddenly they're like:

"Wait… this wasn't as scary as I thought."

Exactly.

You don't need perfect credit to buy a home, you just need clarity and momentum.

$$* * *$$

# ⭐ CHAPTER 4
SAVING SMART: PREPARING WITHOUT PANIC

Let's talk about money — and let's keep it simple.

Because I know the second someone says "down payment," your shoulders tense. But saving for a home doesn't need to be stressful or restrictive. It just needs a plan.

## What You Actually Need to Save

Surprise:

You don't need 20%. You don't even need 10%.

Many buyers qualify with:

• 3% down

• 3.5% down (FHA)

• or even gift funds

Saving smart means understanding **how much** you realistically need, not chasing a random number someone on TikTok yelled about.

## Types of Savings

Think of your savings in buckets:

• Moving costs

• Inspection/appraisal

• Down payment

• Closing costs

• Emergency cushion

You don't need every bucket overflowing — you just need enough to feel supported.

## Where People Get Overwhelmed

They try to do everything at once.

But you?

You're going to prioritize and move one piece at a time. Savings grow with consistency, not stress.

## What Matters Most: Momentum

Saving isn't about how fast you go. It's about direction. Even

$100 a month moves you closer than $0. Small habits turn into big progress.

This chapter helps you ditch the guilt and start saving intentionally — without sacrificing your sanity.

* * *

# ⭐ CHAPTER 5

## PICKING YOUR PERFECT LOAN

Choosing a loan isn't just a financial decision — it's a personality test.

Every loan has its own "vibe," and the right one depends on your goals, your budget, and the stage of life you're in. This chapter helps you understand the most common loan types so you can choose the one that fits you (and your future self) the best.

Think of this as the menu…and I'm the friend who whispers what everything really means so you don't get surprised later.

**Conventional Loans: The Classic Option**

Conventional loans are the "steady, reliable, does-their-chores" type. They're not flashy, but they're solid — and they work beautifully for buyers with decent credit and stable income.

**Great for you if:**

• You have good credit

• You plan to put at least 3% down

• You want competitive rates

• You like flexibility

**Why people love them:**

PMI (private mortgage insurance) can fall off once you hit 20% equity — which means your payment can go *down* over time. That's always a win.

## FHA Loans: The Friendly Helper

### *(Federal Housing Administration)*

FHA loans are like the supportive friend who says, "It's okay, I've got you."

They're designed for buyers who are still building credit or who need a more flexible path into homeownership.

**Great for you if:**

• Your credit is lower

• You want 3.5% down

• You need more forgiving guidelines

• You want a smoother approval path

**Why people choose FHA:**

It opens doors that might otherwise stay closed — especially for first-time buyers.

**But keep this in mind:**

FHA has MIP for life in most cases, which means your mortgage insurance doesn't drop off unless you refinance later.

## VA Loans: The Best Loan in America (if you qualify)

### *(Veterans Affairs)*

If you're a veteran, active-duty service member, or eligible spouse — the VA loan is a gift.

And I truly mean that.

**Great for you if:**

• You're eligible through military service

• You want zero down

• You love low interest rates

• You want no monthly mortgage insurance

This loan can save you tens of thousands of dollars over time. If you qualify — this is almost always your best option.

. . .

## USDA Loans: For Homes with Wide Open Spaces

### *(United States Department of Agriculture)*

The USDA loan is for buyers who want that peaceful, "I hear crickets" life.

It's location-based, with zero-down benefits for rural and suburban properties.

**Great for you if:**

• You're considering a USDA-eligible area

• You want 0% down

• You like the idea of lower upfront costs

USDA loans have income limits and geographical boundaries, so not every home qualifies — but it's a hidden gem worth checking.

## Jumbo Loans: For Higher-Priced Homes

Jumbo loans cover homes that exceed the standard loan limits.

They're like the VIP section — same mortgages, just bigger numbers.

**Great for you if:**

• You're buying above the conforming limit

• You have strong credit

• Your income can support a higher payment

• You prefer one large loan instead of layering financing

Rates can vary, but this product makes high-value homes more accessible than most people think.

## ITIN Loans

One of the most empowering programs out there.

These loans are designed for borrowers who **don't have a Social Security number** but *do* have an ITIN and file taxes with it.

If you live here, work here, pay taxes here, and want to buy a home — an ITIN loan gives you that opportunity. They often require a larger down payment (10–20%), but they make homeownership possible for buyers who are often told "no" when the real answer should be "yes, with the right loan."

## Foreign National Loans

This program is for non-U.S. residents who want to purchase property in the United States — usually for investment, vacation, or part-time use.

You don't need U.S. credit or a Social Security number;

lenders look at international income, bank letters, and a larger down payment (usually 20–30%).

In other words: you can absolutely buy a home here even if you live abroad.

## Adjustable-Rate Mortgages (ARMs): A Strategy, Not a Gamble

An ARM isn't something to fear — it's a planning tool.

You get a lower fixed rate for a set number of years (like 5, 7, or 10), and after that the rate can adjust.

### Great for you if:

• You plan to move before the adjustment

• You're remodeling and refinancing later

• You want a lower starting payment

• You understand the timeline

ARMs are all about strategy. When used wisely, they can save you a lot of money upfront.

## Interest-Only Loans: Not for Everyone, But Amazing for the Right Buyer

Interest-only loans let you pay *just* the interest for a set period.

It keeps payments low in the beginning — but requires discipline.

**Great for you if:**

• You want maximum cash flow

• You're buying a short-term property

• You know your income will rise

• You're a strategic investor

These aren't for brand-new buyers, but in the right hands?

Powerful.

**How to Choose the Loan That Fits YOU**

Here's the truth:

There's no "best" loan — only the best one for *your* situation.

Ask yourself:

• What's my long-term plan for this home?

• How long do I expect to stay?

• What payment makes me comfortable?

• Do I need flexibility, or structure?

• Am I optimizing for the lowest payment, the lowest rate, or the lowest down payment?

Your loan is part of your overall life strategy — not just a financial product.

## The Mindset Shift

Choosing a loan is about alignment — not perfection.

You're not looking for the loan that impresses people or sounds fancy.

You're looking for the loan that supports your goals, protects your budget, and moves you closer to the life you want.

When you choose a loan intentionally, every part of the home buying journey feels smoother and less overwhelming.

And guess what?

You're already ahead of most buyers — because now you understand the options clearly.

\* \* \*

# ⭐ CHAPTER 6

## THE PRE-APPROVAL POWER MOVE

Using the same Speaks Human System™, here's the simple version of how this works…

Getting pre-approved is not just paperwork — it's your power move. It's what separates "I'm thinking about buying a home" from "I'm ready." And trust me, sellers and realtors can feel the difference.

Pre-approval gives you clarity, confidence, and leverage. It tells the world:

**"I'm prepared, I'm serious, and I know my numbers."**

Without it, you're basically shopping blind.

### What Pre-Approval Really Means

A pre-approval is a lender reviewing your financial life and saying,

"Based on what we see today, we feel comfortable lending you up to this amount."

It's not a guarantee — nothing is final until underwriting — but it's the closest you can get before signing a contract.

It's also the difference between being taken seriously and being treated like another "maybe."

## Why It Matters More Than You Think

Pre-approval is your reality check and your confidence boost wrapped into one.

Once you see your numbers, the guessing stops. Instead of wondering, you *know* what you can afford comfortably, what fits your lifestyle, and what price range will set you up for success instead of stress.

It also gives you speed.

When you find "the one," you can make an offer immediately instead of scrambling to gather documents while someone else gets the house.

Pre-approval is about walking into the process with your feet planted firmly on the ground instead of tiptoeing.

. . .

## The Documents You'll Need

(buyers ALWAYS screenshot this part)

• Last 2 years of tax returns

• Last 2 years of W-2s or 1099s

• Recent pay stubs

• Bank statements

• Photo ID

• Any documents showing additional income (pension, social security, alimony, child support, 401k)

## Pre-Qualification vs. Pre-Approval

These two get confused constantly, and the difference matters.

A pre-qualification is based on what you *tell* the lender, not what you prove. It's quick and convenient but not reliable.

A pre-approval is based on actual documents.

It's verified, trustworthy, and the only thing sellers want to see.

Think of pre-qualification like checking symptoms online…

and pre-approval like going to an actual doctor.

One gives you ideas.

The other gives you answers.

## Your Approval Amount vs. Your Comfort Amount

Just because a lender says you *can* afford a certain amount doesn't mean that number fits your real life.

Your true budget comes from how you feel when you imagine the payment — not the maximum you qualify for.

Ask yourself:

"Does this payment feel comfortable?

Or does it feel like I'll be eating rice and beans until further notice?"

You want breathing room.

You want joy.

You want a home that feels good — not one that keeps you up at night.

## What NOT to Do During Pre-Approval

• Don't open new credit

• Don't finance a car

• Don't make large unexplained deposits

• Don't change jobs without checking with your lender

• Don't max out credit cards

• Don't co-sign anything

## How Long Pre-Approval Lasts

Most pre-approvals last 60 to 90 days.

If that window closes before you find the right home, refreshing it is easy. We update documents, check for changes, and move on.

This isn't a race — it's a process.

## Why Rates May Change

The rate you see on your pre-approval is not the rate you're guaranteed. Rates move daily — sometimes hourly — based on market conditions.

This doesn't mean anything is wrong.

It's just how mortgages work.

Your rate gets locked when you're under contract, not during pre-approval.

## The Mindset Shift

Pre-approval isn't about restrictions — it's about clarity.

When you know your real numbers, everything becomes easier. You'll walk into showings with confidence instead of hesitation. You'll write offers without second-guessing yourself. You'll understand what fits your life and what doesn't.

Pre-approval is the moment your dream becomes a plan — and that plan becomes a home.

\* \* \*

# CHAPTER 7

## FROM BROWSING TO BUYING: SHOPPING WITHOUT LOSING YOUR MIND

Let's be real: House shopping is fun… until it isn't. One day you're like: "OMG this one has a pool!" And the next day you're like: "Why are these houses either perfect… or terrifying?"

Welcome to the emotional rollercoaster of home shopping. But don't worry — I'm here to help you ride it without motion sickness.

### Step 1: Know Your Non-Negotiables

Before you step into a single showing, write down:

• MUST haves

• NICE to haves

• ABSOLUTELY NOTs

This keeps you grounded.

You're not going to just "end up" buying a house because the light fixtures were cute.

## Step 2: Look Beyond the Pretty Stuff

Pretty kitchens are great.

But look at:

• Roof age

• AC age

• Electrical

• Plumbing

• Foundation

• Neighborhood trends

These are the things that save you money later.

## Step 3: Don't Let One "No" Break You

Sometimes the house you love gets snapped up by someone else.

Or the inspection reveals termites with their own mortgage.

It's okay.

Rejection is redirection in real estate. Your home is out there — let the wrong ones go.

## Step 4: Keep Your Feelings + Math Balanced

Your heart will fall in love. Your calculator will tap you on the shoulder like:

"Hi. I'd like to remind you that the HOA is $700."

Both matter.

We want heart + math, not one or the other.

\* \* \*

## ⭐ CHAPTER 8

### FROM OFFER TO KEYS: THE EMOTIONAL MARATHON

Making an offer on a home is the moment everything starts to feel *real*. Up until now, it's been dreaming, scrolling, comparing, imagining…

But once you write that offer? You're officially in the game.

This chapter walks you through what happens from the moment you say "Let's make an offer" to the moment you're standing in your new home with keys in hand.

No stress. No confusion. Just a clear path.

### Step 1 — Writing the Offer

Your realtor will help you structure the offer, but here's what actually matters:

• The price you're offering

- Your earnest deposit

- Your closing timeline

- Any contingencies you're requesting

Each of these details tells the seller something about you — your seriousness, your preparation, and your ability to close. A strong offer isn't just about the highest number. It's about showing that you're reliable, ready, and the kind of buyer who won't disappear halfway through the process.

## Step 2 — The Seller's Response

Once your offer is submitted, the seller can:

1 Accept

2 Counter

3 Reject

4 Ignore it completely (yes, this happens)

A counteroffer is normal. Don't take it personally — it's not rejection; it's negotiation. Think of it like dancing: someone leads, someone follows, you both adjust until it feels right. If the seller counters, your realtor will help you respond in a way that keeps you competitive without overextending yourself.

## Step 3 — You're Under Contract! Now What?

Once both parties agree and sign, you're officially "Under Contract." This is where the real work begins, but don't worry, there's a rhythm to it.

The first few days typically involve:

• Paying your escrow deposit

• Ordering the inspection

• Ordering the appraisal

• Finalizing your loan application

• Sending updated documents to your lender

It feels like a lot at once, but you move through it step by step. And I'll be right here explaining what everything means.

## Step 4 — The Inspection

The inspection is your opportunity to understand the home on a deeper level. Think of it like a first date — you're learning what's beneath the surface.

Your inspector will check:

• the roof

• plumbing

• electrical system

• HVAC

• appliances

• structure

• overall condition

This is not about perfection. No home is flawless, not even brand new construction. It's about understanding what you're buying and what (if anything) needs to be negotiated or repaired.

## Step 5 — The Appraisal

The appraisal determines the home's market value. It protects you *and* the lender — nobody wants to overpay.

If the appraisal comes in at or above the purchase price, amazing.

If it comes in low, there are options:

• renegotiate the price

• meet in the middle

• pay the difference if you still love the home

Low appraisals are frustrating but fixable — there's always a path forward.

## Step 6 — Loan Processing & Underwriting

While you're doing inspections and appraisals, your lender is working behind the scenes.

The loan processor collects and organizes your documents. Underwriting reviews everything to make sure the loan meets guidelines.

This part can feel slow or repetitive — you may be asked for updated pay stubs, letters of explanation, or extra documentation.

It's not personal. It's standard. It's simply how lenders make sure your approval stays on track.

### Step 7 — Conditions & Clear to Close

Underwriters almost never approve a file with zero conditions.

Expect a few things like:

• updated statements

• explanations for deposits

• clarification on employment

• insurance documents

Once those conditions are met, the magic words appear:

**Clear to Close.**

This means the lender has approved everything, the numbers are finalized, and you're almost at the finish line.

Clear to Close is the "green light" of the mortgage world.

. . .

## Step 8 — Closing Disclosure

Before closing, you'll receive your Closing Disclosure, which outlines all your final numbers:

• loan amount

• interest rate

• monthly payment

• taxes

• insurance

• closing costs

• cash to close

You must receive this at least three days before closing — it's a federal rule. Review it closely. If anything looks off, ask questions. Now is the time to clarify, not at the closing table.

## Step 9 — Closing Day

This is the moment everyone looks forward to. You'll sign documents, receive copies, confirm your final numbers, and once everything is recorded…

You get the keys.

This is the moment where the stress melts away and the

excitement takes over. It's the moment you've been working toward since Chapter 1.

Your new chapter officially begins.

## The Mindset Shift

From offer to keys, the process can feel big — but it's not meant to overwhelm you. Each step has a purpose. Each moment moves you closer to home. When you understand the flow, the stress disappears and the confidence grows. Buying a home isn't just a transaction — it's a transition.

And now you know exactly how to navigate it.

* * *

# CHAPTER 9

## WELCOME HOME: WHAT HAPPENS AFTER YOU CLOSE

This chapter is here so you don't panic 48 hours after closing thinking:

"Why did my lender ask me for documents for three months and now... nothing?"

Welcome to homeownership — the quiet part.

### Your First Payments

You typically skip the first month's payment. So if you close in April, your first payment is June 1. That's normal. No need to call the FBI.

### Protect Your Home

• Get your homestead exemption

• Set up utilities

• Change locks

- Check air filters

- Deep clean

- Set reminders for maintenance

These tiny things save big money later.

## Don't Make Big Financial Moves Yet

No new cars.

No new credit cards.

No "I'm a homeowner, let me celebrate with a $4,000 couch" purchase.

Let everything settle for 30–60 days.

## Celebrate Your Win

Homeownership is a milestone. You worked for this. Take a minute to breathe and appreciate what you've accomplished.

You deserve it.

\* \* \*

# ⭐ CHAPTER 10

## HOMEOWNER HABITS: KEEPING YOUR HOME + FINANCES HEALTHY

Owning a home isn't the finish line — it's the start of a whole new chapter. But it doesn't have to be stressful. Just like your health, your home needs a little check-up now and then.

### Habit 1: Track Your Equity

Every year, take a moment to check:

• your loan balance

• your home value

• your equity

You'll be surprised how quickly it grows.

### Habit 2: Maintain, Maintain, Maintain

Little things become big things when ignored.

Do this regularly:

• AC filter changes

• Roof checks

• Plumbing checks

• Termite inspections

A $40 filter change can prevent a $3,000 repair.

## Habit 3: Review Your Insurance

Once a year, call your insurer and ask:

"Am I overpaying?" You'd be shocked how many people save hundreds with a quick review.

## Habit 4: Revisit Your Goals

Your home should grow with your life.

Ask yourself:

• Do I want to refinance?

• Do I want to invest?

• Do I want to renovate?

• Do I want to move?

The better your habits, the stronger your financial future.

\* \* \*

# ⭐ CHAPTER 11

## REFINANCING, RENOVATING & YOUR HOME EQUITY: YOUR SECRET WEALTH TOOLS

Your home comes with a secret superpower: **equity**.

It quietly grows in the background — like a savings account you didn't have to remember to transfer money into. One day you check your home value and suddenly you're thinking:

"Wait… was my house working overtime while I slept?"

Yes. Yes, it was.

Welcome to the financial glow-up no one warned you about.

This chapter shows you how to use that equity wisely — without turning your home into an ATM or starring in the next episode of *Financial Disasters: Renovation Edition.*

· · ·

## Your Home Equity: The Money You Built Without Trying

Your equity is simply the difference between your home's value and your loan balance. Sometimes it grows because you paid down your mortgage. Sometimes it grows because the market is in a good mood. Sometimes it grows because your neighbor redid their kitchen and suddenly everyone's homes are worth more.

Whatever the reason, equity is real wealth — and you get to decide how to use it.

## Refinancing: A Reset Button for Grown-Ups

A refinance is basically your mortgage asking,

"Would you like to try that again, but smarter this time?"

You replace your current loan with a new one, usually because you want a better rate, a better payment, or a better structure. It's like updating your phone — you don't always need to, but wow does life get smoother when you do.

There are two main flavors of refinancing, and each one has its own personality.

## Rate-and-Term Refinance: The Polished, Responsible One

This refinance is all about efficiency. You're not pulling cash out — you're simply improving what you already have. Maybe your rate is too high. Maybe your payment feels tight. Maybe you're ready to drop mortgage insurance.

A rate-and-term refinance is the "let's clean this up" option. Quiet, simple, and shockingly effective.

## Cash-Out Refinance: When You Need Money for Something Important

A cash-out refinance lets you convert some of your equity into actual money. The key word here is **important** — home improvements, paying off high-interest credit cards, consolidating debt, investing in your future. Not ideal for things like jet skis, spontaneous vacations, or "I saw it on TikTok and now I need it" moments.

It's a powerful tool… when used with intention.

## Renovating: The Fastest Way to Boost Your Value (and Your Happiness)

If you've ever watched HGTV for six minutes, you already know a good renovation can skyrocket your home's value. A new kitchen adds appeal. A fresh bathroom adds confidence. Updated flooring adds that "my house suddenly feels cleaner" feeling.

Renovations are fabulous when you focus on upgrades that add value. If your vision board includes a built-in aquarium or a medieval-style wine dungeon, let's pause and breathe.

Renovate with strategy, not chaos.

## HELOC: The Flexible, Don't-Abuse-Me Option

A HELOC is a home equity line of credit — basically a credit card backed by your house, except way smarter and with better rates. You don't have to use it — but it's there if you need it. Perfect for unexpected repairs, calculated opportunities, or bigger expenses that pop up. Not perfect for people who spend money the second they see it.

Use wisely. Respectfully. Like a well-behaved emergency fund with superpowers.

## Which Option Fits Your Life?

Choosing between a refinance, a HELOC, or renovations depends on your goals.

Ask yourself: Am I trying to **save money**, **access money**, or **grow value**? What will my future self thank me for? Will this move me closer to financial stability or away from it?

If you want to **save money**, rate-and-term is your friend. If you want to **use money**, cash-out or HELOC fits the mission. If you want to **increase value**, renovations are your best investment.

It's not about the "fanciest" option — it's about the smartest one for your life.


## The Mindset Shift

Your home isn't just a place to live — it's a financial engine. It's growing in the background. It's building wealth quietly. It's giving you options without demanding attention.

When you learn how to use equity with intention, you stop reacting to life and start designing it. Your home is more than shelter. It's stability, growth, and opportunity — all wrapped into one.

\* \* \*

# ⭐ CHAPTER 12

## CHANGE, CHALLENGES & MORTGAGE MOVES

Life has a talent for surprising us at the worst possible moments. You can have a plan, a timeline, a budget, and a color-coded spreadsheet... and suddenly you're staring at your mortgage statement thinking, "Well, this wasn't in the brochure." But here's the good news: your mortgage can adjust to your life just as much as your life adjusts to your mortgage. You have options. More than most people realize.

Sometimes those options show up quietly — a job change, a big bill, a new family dynamic — and sometimes they crash through the door like a toddler with a marker. Either way, this chapter is about giving you clarity, stability, and just enough humor to stay sane while making the smartest moves for your financial life.

### When Life Shifts, Your Mortgage Can Too

People often tell themselves they're "stuck" with the mortgage they signed. Not true. Mortgages aren't tattoos. They're more like long-term relationships: mostly stable, sometimes complicated, and occasionally in need of a serious conversation.

As your life evolves, your mortgage sometimes needs to evolve with you. Whether you're earning more, earning less, changing careers, adjusting your family structure, or just becoming a different version of yourself... your home is part of that journey. You don't have to force your life to fit your loan — you can adjust your loan to fit your life.

## When Big Expenses Arrive Without Knocking

We all know those moments. The AC dies during a heatwave. The roof suddenly decides it's done participating in society. The car needs repairs that cost more than the car is worth. Or your pet eats something that should never have been in their mouth to begin with.

Big surprise expenses can shake your budget fast, but they don't have to shake your stability. This is where options like refinancing, restructuring, or tapping into equity with a HELOC can help you manage the situation without spiraling into stress. These tools exist for times exactly like this: not for fun, not for luxury, but for life being life.

## When Income Changes Change Everything

Whether you're celebrating a raise, navigating a job loss, switching careers, or stepping into the unpredictable world of self-employment, any shift in income impacts the way your finances feel. A raise can open new possibilities. A job loss can bring real fear. Self-employment comes with both freedom and paperwork that looks like it was designed by a medieval scribe.

Whatever your income story looks like right now, you're not locked into your old mortgage terms. You might adjust your budget. You might refinance. You might simply pause and let life settle before making a big move. The important thing is knowing your mortgage isn't a rigid structure — it's flexible enough to support your next chapter.

## When Relationships Change the Equation

Divorce, separation, and major relationship shifts come with emotional weight — and the financial side can feel just as heavy. If a mortgage is involved, it can feel overwhelming fast. But in reality, there are several paths forward: refinancing into one person's name, selling and splitting the equity, or restructuring in a way that creates fairness and peace.

These transitions are hard, but your mortgage doesn't have to add to the chaos. You have practical, compassionate options — and you don't have to face them alone.

. . .

## When Health or Family Emergencies Shift Priorities

Medical issues, family emergencies, and caregiving responsibilities have a way of rearranging priorities overnight. Suddenly, the mortgage isn't the main character — your wellbeing is. During these moments, your home should support you, not overwhelm you. Adjusting your mortgage, refinancing to lower payments, or accessing equity isn't a setback; it's a strategy. One that gives you room to breathe while life demands your attention elsewhere.

## When You Simply Need a Fresh Start

Sometimes the reason isn't dramatic — it's simply honest. You've outgrown your home. You want a different neighborhood. You're ready for a new lifestyle. You want something brighter, quieter, calmer, bigger, smaller, closer, farther — whatever speaks to your next season.

There's nothing impulsive about wanting a fresh start. Growth isn't a red flag. It's a sign you're paying attention to your life.

## How to Know When It's Time for a Mortgage Move

Here are the quick-hit questions — woven right into your flow — that help you understand whether something needs to shift:

Does your mortgage support your life right now, or does it feel like you're constantly adjusting your life to support the mortgage? Are you stressed because your payment is too high, or simply ready for something that feels more aligned with your future? Would changing your loan increase your financial stability? Or your peace? Or both?

Your answers are your guide. They're rarely dramatic. They're usually honest, quiet, and clear.

## The Mindset Shift

Your mortgage is not a trap, and you are not "stuck." You're allowed to adjust, pivot, and evolve. You're allowed to make financial decisions that protect your wellbeing. You're allowed to choose the option that supports your life today — not the one you chose five years ago under completely different circumstances.

When challenges show up, you don't panic — you strategize. When life changes, you reassess. When something unexpected happens, you adapt. That's not instability. It's wisdom.

Your home is part of your life story, and you get to decide how the next chapter reads.

* * *

# ★ CHAPTER 13

## INVESTING IN REAL ESTATE & INVESTOR-FRIENDLY LOAN PROGRAMS

*How Real People Build Real Wealth (Even Without W-2s or "Perfect" Credit)*

Let's talk about real estate investing — the topic that makes some people excited... and others immediately start sweating. Here's the truth:

**Investing isn't just for rich people.**

It isn't only for people with perfect credit, giant savings accounts, or W-2 jobs with matching lunchboxes. Regular people invest in real estate every day. And many of them started exactly where you are: curious, unsure, a little intimidated, but very ready to change their financial future

So let's break this down simply, clearly, and in a way that makes you feel *empowered*, not overwhelmed.

. . .

## Why People Invest in Real Estate

People invest for one (or all) of these reasons:

- **Monthly cash flow**
- **Long-term appreciation**
- **Tax advantages**
- **Equity growth**
- **Financial security**
- **Retirement planning**
- **Generational wealth**

And the best part?

Real estate lets you build wealth using something called **leverage** — meaning you can use the bank's money (not just yours) to buy an asset that pays *you*. That's why real estate is one of the fastest paths to wealth for everyday people.

## Investment Types (The Lily Edition)

### ✓ Long-Term Rentals

The classic. A tenant pays rent, you build equity and wealth over time. Predictable and stable.

### ✓ Short-Term Rentals (Airbnb)

Higher potential income, higher management. Great in the right markets.

## ✓ **Multifamily (2–4 Units)**

*This is my favorite for first-time investors.*

Live in one unit, rent the others → let your tenants pay your mortgage. This is called **house hacking** — and it's how many people start investing with very little down.

## ✓ **Fix-and-Flip**

Buy it ugly, make it pretty, sell it fast. More risk, bigger reward.

Not for beginners unless you love stress and Home Depot.

## **What Most People Get Wrong**

Most people think they can't invest because their tax returns don't show "enough", they don't have a traditional job, they write off expenses as business owners, they aren't perfect on paper, their credit isn't flawless.

Let me tell you something important:

**There are loan programs made specifically for you.**

Yes — YOU. Not perfect you. Not pretend-you. Actual you.

These programs exist to help everyday people become investors, even if they don't qualify the "old-school" way.

Welcome to the good part.

. . .

## Investor-Friendly Loan Programs (That Most People Don't Know Exist)

These programs are the key to making investing possible for modern buyers.

Let's break them down.

## DSCR Loans (Debt Service Coverage Ratio Loans)

*The investor's best friend.*

A DSCR loan doesn't care about your personal income.

Read that again.

DSCR lenders care about **the property's income**, not yours.

**Here's the rule:**

**If the rent covers the mortgage, the loan works.**

That's it. Mic drop.

This is perfect for:

• business owners

• self-employed borrowers

• commission earners

• people who reinvest heavily

• buyers with strong cash flow

• anyone building a rental portfolio

If a rental property can pay for itself, lenders are usually happy.

DSCR gives you the freedom to invest even if your tax return looks like you made $4 and a sandwich last year (hello, write-offs 😅).

## Bank Statement Loans

*The self-employed superstar.*

Bank Statement loans qualify you using — you guessed it — your **bank statements**, not your tax returns.

This program is made for:

• entrepreneurs

• small business owners

• freelancers

• gig workers

• realtors

• commission-based earners

• anyone whose real income doesn't show up on paper

Lenders look at:

• 12 or 24 months of deposits

• your true cash flow

• your business stability

This is HUGE for people whose tax returns don't reflect their real buying power because of write-offs. If money is consistently coming in, you can qualify.

### Why These Programs Matter

Because for many people, these two programs are the difference between: **"I wish I could invest someday..."** and **"I own a rental property now."**

The truth is, most investors don't start perfect. They start *smart.* They use tools that match their real lives, real income, and real goals.

DSCR loans and Bank Statement loans are those tools.

### How Real People Build Real Wealth

Here's the pattern I've seen again and again:

Someone buys one property... then they use DSCR to buy another. Then another. Then they refinance one. Maybe they house-hack a duplex. Maybe they convert a property into a short-term rental.

Suddenly — with small, consistent steps — they've built a portfolio. Not because they were wealthy. Not because they had perfect credit. Not because they waited until everything was "ideal." But because they took the first step with the right program.

## The Mindset That Changes Everything

Real estate investing isn't about being fearless.

It's about being informed.

Once you understand:

• cash flow

• equity

• appreciation

• creative loan programs

• how lenders think

• how numbers work

…it stops being scary and starts being exciting. And YOU now know more than most people ever will.

Your next step?

Choose the strategy that fits your life and take action — even small action.

* * *

## ⭐ CHAPTER 14

### WHEN TO SELL, WHEN TO STAY & HOW TO DECIDE WITHOUT REGRET

Selling your home isn't like unfriending someone on social media — it's more like deciding whether to stay in a good relationship or explore what else is out there. It's emotional, it's practical, it's occasionally dramatic, and it often begins with you staring at your house thinking, "Is it me... or is it you?"

This chapter gives you the clarity to make the decision confidently, without guilt, panic, or the haunting thought that you might make the wrong move. Because when you approach the choice intentionally, it's never the wrong one.

**Start with Your "Why"**

Before you open Zillow or start mentally packing boxes, pause and ask yourself why you're even thinking about moving. Are you craving more space? Less space? A better commute? A different environment? Or do you just need a change because life feels like it's pushing you into a new season?

Sometimes your reasons are practical — a growing family, a new job, or a lifestyle shift. And sometimes they're quieter: boredom, restlessness, or the feeling that your life has outgrown your walls. If the reason is emotional, it doesn't mean it's invalid. It simply means you may want to look for the *real* need underneath: Do you truly need a new home, or just a new layout, new paint, or new energy? You'd be surprised how often people rediscover their love for a home after adjusting a few things.

## Run the Numbers (This Is Where the Honesty Lives)

Now let's talk money — because even the best emotional decision needs financial clarity. Selling isn't just "I'll list it and see what happens." It comes with real costs. Realtor fees, closing costs, moving expenses, repairs, staging — it all adds up faster than you'd expect.

Once you subtract what you owe and the cost of selling, what's left is your **net equity**. That number is your budget for the next chapter. If it helps you move into a better home, pay down debt, reach a financial milestone, or secure more stability, then selling might make perfect sense. If the number leaves you frustrated or limited, staying put a little longer might be the wiser move — even if it's not the most exciting one.

## Consider Your Lifestyle — Not Just the House

Sometimes the decision isn't about the home at all. It's about the life you're living inside it. Does your home still support the life you have today — not the one you had when you bought it? Does it make daily life easier, or does it frustrate you? Could you make the home feel new again with a renovation, a fresh setup, or a few intentional updates?

We tend to underestimate how much our environment shapes our mood and mindset. A refreshed space can feel like a whole new chapter without a single moving box. But if you're constantly rearranging things trying to make the home "work," that's your sign. Homes don't need to be perfect — but they should fit your life, your energy, and your next season.

## Know When Moving Is the Right Call

Sometimes the truth is obvious: you've outgrown your home. Your rooms feel small. Your commute is draining you. The stairs are suddenly rude. The yard feels like a full-time job. Or maybe you're ready for a lifestyle shift — more land, less maintenance, better schools, or a location that feels more aligned with who you're becoming.

Moving isn't running away — it's choosing what supports your life now. When your environment no longer matches your goals, growth means stepping into something new.

## A Reality Check on Timing

The market will always have opinions: "It's a seller's market," "It's a buyer's market," "Inventory is low," "Rates are high," "Prices are rising," "Prices are settling," and so on.

The truth?

The best time to move is when **your life** aligns with the opportunity — not when the headlines say it's perfect. Markets will always fluctuate. But your needs, your goals, your finances, and your peace of mind matter far more than the news cycle.

## The Mindset Shift

Whether you stay or go, this isn't just a real estate decision — it's a life decision. Your home has held your memories, supported your growth, and carried you through seasons. And whether that chapter continues or closes, the next step will always move you forward.

Selling or staying isn't about trends. It's about truth — the truth of where you are, who you're becoming, and what you want your life to feel like.

Whichever path you choose, do it with intention.

Do it with clarity.

Do it with confidence.

Your home is part of your journey — not the anchor that holds you back.

\* \* \*

# ⭐ CHAPTER 15

## YOUR MORTGAGE MINDSET: CONFIDENCE, CLARITY & WHAT COMES NEXT

Take a breath. Seriously — pause for one second.

You've made it to the end of this book, and that alone says something important about you. You didn't just skim the headlines or scroll past the process. You leaned in. You took the time to understand the pieces, the decisions, the math, the emotions, and the strategy behind one of the biggest milestones of your life.

And now?

You're standing on the other side of the mortgage maze, calmer, wiser, and infinitely more prepared than you were when you opened Chapter 1.

**What You've Really Gained**

Let's be honest — this wasn't just a crash course in interest rates and escrow accounts. You've learned something far bigger: how to take control of your financial life with confidence instead of panic.

You now understand how lenders think and what they look for. You know how to prepare, how to protect your finances, and how to make decisions that move you forward instead of holding you back. You learned how to build wealth one smart step at a time, and how to see your home — not as a finish line — but as a stepping stone.

Most importantly, you learned how to think clearly instead of fearfully.

That skill alone is worth more than any rate drop.

## Putting Your Mortgage Mindset into Action

When you approach homeownership with the right mindset, everything feels different. You start asking better questions. You pause before reacting. You make decisions instead of assumptions. You recognize opportunities instead of red flags disguised as impossible mountains.

You're no longer the person who once Googled "what even is an escrow?" at 11 PM. You've evolved into someone who can explain it to someone else — calmly, clearly, and confidently. That's not just growth. That's mastery.

With the right mindset, you don't need to know everything.

You only need to know enough to make strong, educated choices — and you absolutely do.

## What Comes Next for You?

Your next steps don't have to be dramatic or life-changing. They just need to be intentional.

Maybe your next move is paying off your mortgage a little faster.

Maybe it's buying an investment property and growing your portfolio.

Maybe it's teaching your friends or family what you've learned, so they don't get lost in the process.

Or maybe?

Maybe it's simply enjoying the peace of mind that comes from finally understanding how all of this works.

Whatever your next step looks like, you're not walking into it blindly. You're doing it with clarity — and clarity is the most powerful financial tool you can have.

## The Mindset Moment

Homeownership isn't only about where you live — it's about how you live. It's about creating stability, options, and choices. It's about building a foundation strong enough to support your dreams, your family, your goals, and every version of the life you're building.

And here's the truth:

You didn't just buy a home.

You built a foundation.

You built confidence.

You built knowledge.

You built momentum.

And now you get to use all of it.

Your mortgage is no longer something you fear, avoid, or second-guess. It's something you handle with clarity — and clarity is what builds legacies.

You have everything you need. You always did. Now you simply know how to use it.

# ⭐ CHAPTER 16

## THE MOST COMMON HOMEBUYER QUESTIONS (ANSWERED IN SIMPLE TERMS)

You deserve answers without confusion, judgment, or Googling at 1 a.m.

Here are the questions I get asked the most — answered simply, clearly, and with zero mortgage-robot energy.

### 1. What if I change jobs during the process?

Totally depends on the job change.

✔ Staying in the same field? Usually fine.

✔ Salary → salary? Fine.

✔ Hourly → hourly? Fine.

✔ Salary → commission? We need to talk first.

✔ Job gap longer than 90 days? Depends — but not impossible.

When in doubt: **Ask before you say yes to the new job.**


## 2. Will my loan fall apart if my credit score drops before closing?

Usually **no** — unless it drops dramatically.

Here's how it works:

• We use the score from your initial credit pull.

• If your score drops slightly, it's often still fine.

• If you miss payments or max out a card? Different story.

Rule of thumb:

**Keep your credit quiet and boring until closing.**


## 3. Can I buy a home if I have student loans?

YES.

Student loans do NOT disqualify you.

We just count the monthly payment toward your DTI.

If your payment is:

• Income-based? We use that.

• Deferred? We still count a small amount.

• $0? Lenders have a formula — still workable.

You're not alone — almost every buyer has student loans.

## 4. How long does underwriting really take?

Typical timeline:

### 48 hours to a week.

It feels longer because you're stressed… but underwriting isn't trying to torture you.

Keep your documents ready and your responses quick — this speeds up everything.

## 5. What's the biggest mistake buyers make?

Easy:

### Falling in love with a home before knowing their numbers.

This leads to heartbreak, stress, and existential crisis.

Get pre-approved FIRST.

Shop SECOND.

## 6. Do I need 20% down?

No.

No.

And again: NO.

Modern mortgages let you buy with:

• 3% down (Conventional)

• 3.5% down (FHA)

• 0% down (VA & USDA)

• Or **gift funds**

Don't let old-school rules block your future.


## 7. Can I buy a home with overtime, bonuses, or commission income?

Most of the time, YES — as long as it's consistent and documented.

If it fluctuates, we average it.

If it's brand new, we may need more history.

Every situation has solutions.

Ask early.


## 8. Should I pay off my debt before buying a house?

Maybe… or maybe NOT.

Paying off debt can help your DTI, BUT:

• Don't drain your savings.

• Don't empty your home buying fund.

• Don't create new debt to pay off old debt.

Let your lender run the numbers.

Sometimes **keeping** the cash is smarter.

## 9. When is the "best time" to buy a home?

The best time is when:

• you're financially ready

• the payment fits your budget

• you found a home that works for your lifestyle

The "Perfect Market" is a myth.

Your timing matters more than the headlines.

## 10. What if something goes wrong during the process?

We fix it.

That's it.

Every file has bumps — literally every one.

The power move is asking questions, staying calm, and having a team that supports you.

\* \* \*

## FAQ for Self-Employed Buyers

*Yes — you can buy a home, even with write-offs and spicy tax returns.*

## 1. Do I really need two years of tax returns?

Usually yes — but not always.

If you've been self-employed **for less than two years**, we can sometimes use:

• 1 year of returns

• bank statements

• DSCR (if investing)

• strong cash flow documentation

It's case-by-case, but VERY possible.

## 2. What if my tax returns show low income because I write everything off?

Welcome to the club. 😅

This is exactly why **Bank Statement Loans** exist.

With these programs, we use:

• 12–24 months of deposits

• business cash flow

• your actual income — not your tax return income

Huge advantage for entrepreneurs.

## 3. Are 1099 buyers treated differently from W-2 buyers?

Not worse — just different.

We look at:

• consistency

• stability

• deposit patterns

• business history

If the money is there and steady, you're good.

## 4. Do I have to be incorporated (LLC/S-Corp) to buy a home?

Nope.

Sole proprietors get approved all the time.

## 5. Should I change how I do my taxes if I want to buy soon?

Do NOT make big changes without talking to your lender first.

Sometimes writing off less helps.

Sometimes it hurts.

Let's plan this *strategically*.

* * *

## 🏠 FAQ for First-Time Buyers

*The "talk to me like I'm new" section.*

### 1. What if I don't know my credit score?

We'll pull it for you — no need to panic.

And even if it's lower than expected, there are programs for that.

### 2. How much money do I really need to buy a home?

Way less than people think.

Many first-timers use:

• 3% down

• 3.5% down

• gift funds

• down payment assistance (state/county programs)

You don't need 20% unless you want to.

## 3. What if I'm scared of asking "dumb" questions?

There are no dumb questions.

Mortgages are confusing because nobody teaches this in school.

Ask everything.

Ask twice.

Ask ten times.

You're supposed to.

## 4. What if I fall in love with a house that's above my price range?

It's normal — it happens a lot.

Think of it like dating someone who's great… but lives three hours away.

You *could* make it work, but it requires sacrifice.

Stick to your comfort range.

. . .

## 5. What if I get cold feet?

Totally normal.

Buying a home is life-changing.

Fear doesn't mean you're not ready — it means you care.

\* \* \*

## 🏚 FAQ for Investors

*Short, powerful, and extremely useful.*

## 1. Do I need great credit to invest?

Better credit = better rates, yes.

But DSCR programs often approve with **620–640+**.

## 2. How much down payment do investors need?

Most investors put **15–25% down**, but:

• DSCR loans

• bank statement loans

• multifamily owner-occupied loans

…can reduce that significantly.

. . .

## 3. Can I use rental income to qualify?

Yes — that's literally what DSCR was built for.

If the rent covers the mortgage, you're halfway there.

## 4. Can I buy a rental as my first property?

YES — especially a duplex, triplex, or fourplex.

Live in one unit → rent the others → build equity faster.

It's called house hacking, and it's brilliant.

## 5. How soon can I buy another rental after the first one?

Immediately — if your numbers support it.

Investing is all about math, strategy, and lender guidelines.

## 🌴 FAQ for Florida Buyers

*Florida is a different world — literally and financially.*

### 1. Why are property taxes so different here?

Because:

• Florida has **no income tax**,

• taxes vary county-to-county,

• homestead exemptions save $$$,

• and reassessments happen when you buy.

Lee County and Miami-Dade are not twins.


## 2. Do I need hurricane insurance?

If you're in a wind zone: yes.

If you're in a flood zone: also yes.

Florida insurance is… an experience. 😅

A good insurance agent is key.


## 3. Why are HOA fees so high in Florida?

Because we have:

• pools

• gyms

• landscaping

• reserves

• gates

• maintenance

• tropical weather

• and some buildings that are older than your parents

Amenities + weather = higher dues.

## 4. Should I be worried about special assessments?

You should be aware — especially in older condos.

Ask your realtor for:

• condo budget

• reserves

• pending assessments

• past assessments

Knowledge = power.

## 5. Why does everyone talk about flood zones?

Because one wrong flood zone can double your insurance.

Always check flood maps before making an offer.

# ⭐ CHAPTER 17

## THE TOP 10 MISTAKES BUYERS MAKE AND HOW TO AVOID THEM

Almost every buyer makes the *same* mistakes — not because they're careless, but because nobody teaches this stuff in a way that makes sense. Consider this your "avoid the drama" chapter. Learn these mistakes → save money, stress, and sanity.

## ✖ 1. Falling in Love With a House Before Getting Pre-Approved

I know, I know. The kitchen backsplash made you feel something.

But falling in love too early is the fastest path to heartbreak.

**Fix:**

Get pre-approved FIRST so your heart and your budget are on the same team.

. . .

## ✖ 2. Shopping at the Top of Their Budget

Just because you *can* qualify for $450k doesn't mean you want to pay the monthly bill for $450k.

**Fix:**

Choose the number you want to live with — not the one you barely qualify for.

## ✖ 3. Opening New Credit During the Process

New car? New credit card? New furniture?

Congratulations — but not during underwriting.

**Fix:**

Keep your credit quiet until you get your keys.

## ✖ 4. Not Reading the HOA Rules

Yes, the pool is cute.

But the HOA might not allow:

• rentals

• pets

• trucks

• certain renovations

• parking where you *think* you can park

**Fix:**

Read the rules before you fall in love.

## ✖ 5. Not Accounting for Closing Costs

Down payment ≠ total cost.

**Fix:**

Estimate 2–5% for closing costs depending on your market.

## ✖ 6. Ignoring Future Costs (Like Insurance & Taxes)

Your mortgage isn't just principal + interest.

It's also taxes, insurance, and sometimes HOA fees.

**Fix:**

Always look at the **total monthly payment**, not the price tag.

## ✖ 7. Letting Fear Make Decisions

Fear makes buyers freeze. Or settle. Or overpay.

**Fix:**

Take emotion out of the math, and math out of the emotions.

Use both — they need each other.

## ✖ 8. Skipping the Inspection

I know you love the house. But hidden problems don't care.

**Fix:**

Always get an inspection. Always.

Even on new construction.

## ✖ 9. Having Unrealistic Expectations

There is no "perfect" home.

There is a "perfect for your life right now" home.

**Fix:**

Focus on structure, neighborhood, layout — not the paint color.

## ✖ 10. Waiting for the "Perfect Market Moment"

Trying to time the market is basically guessing.

**Fix:**

The right time to buy is when **your** life aligns with a home and a payment you're comfortable with.

**"Avoid these mistakes and you'll instantly be ahead of 80% of buyers."**

\* \* \*

# CHAPTER 18
## SELF-EMPLOYED BUYER MINI-GUIDE

Buying a home when you're self-employed feels a little like showing up to a party where everyone else has name tags… and you're over here explaining three LLCs, two revenue streams, and why your "write-offs" are not the whole story.

But don't panic — you're not alone.

Millions of self-employed buyers get approved every year, and you can absolutely be one of them.

You just need clarity, preparation, and a lender who understands that being your own boss does **not** make you risky — it just makes you different.

Let's break this down the Lily way: clear, human, and without the mortgage guilt trip.

**Understanding How Lenders See Self-Employment**

Here's the part most buyers never hear:

Lenders love entrepreneurs.

They just need to understand your income — and self-employed income takes a little more decoding.

When you're W-2, income is simple.

When you're self-employed, lenders analyze earnings after expenses, stability, tax patterns, and whether your business looks like it's thriving or surviving.

It's not judgment.

It's just math — mixed with a little curiosity.


## The Tax Return Truth Bomb

This is the hardest part for most self-employed buyers:

What you *tell* the IRS is what lenders use.

If you write off everything — the laptop, the mileage, the desk, the conference trip, the planner, the dog that "guards the home office" — your taxable income gets smaller... which feels great at tax time but not so great when you're trying to qualify for a mortgage.

This doesn't mean you shouldn't take deductions.

It just means you need to balance tax savings with future homeownership plans.

Think "smart," not "savage."

. . .

## Consistency Is Queen

Self-employed buyers don't need perfect numbers.

They need consistent numbers.

Lenders want to see that your income is steady, rising, or at least not falling off a cliff.

If the past two years show stability — or growth — you're in great shape.

If one year dipped, don't panic.

Maybe you paused work for health reasons, maternity leave, COVID disruptions, family care, or a business pivot.

Those stories matter.

Your lender can explain them — honestly and confidently — as long as they're documented.

## Bank Statements Matter More Than You Think

When you're self-employed, the lender isn't just looking at your tax returns.

They're looking at your bank statements to understand:

• How your business cash flows

• How you pay yourself

• How stable deposits are

• Whether the business is healthy behind the scenes

Don't let this scare you.

Think of it as lenders getting the full picture — not the cropped version.

## Your Business Doesn't Need to Be Fancy

You don't need a complicated corporation or perfect book-keeping to qualify for a mortgage.

You can be:

• a sole proprietor

• an independent contractor

• a 1099 freelancer

• an LLC

• a one-woman empire

• a "my office is wherever my laptop is" entrepreneur

What matters is that your income can be verified.

Success does not need to look corporate.

## Common Myths (Let's Clear These Up)

**"I need two full years of tax returns or I'm doomed."**

Not always. There *are* programs that accept one year — depending on the lender and your business structure.

**"Write-offs ruin everything."**

They don't. They just reduce qualifying income, which means you'll want to plan intentionally.

**"Lenders don't trust self-employed buyers."**

False. Lenders love numbers, not labels.

**"I make good money but don't show it on taxes — so I can't buy."**

You can. You just may need a non-traditional program.

## When Traditional Loans Don't Fit: Special Programs for Entrepreneurs

If your tax return income is too low because of deductions (welcome to the club), there are flexible programs that might be a better fit:

### Bank Statement Loans

Instead of tax returns, lenders use your bank deposits to calculate income.

Perfect for entrepreneurs with healthy revenue but aggressive write-offs.

## 1099-Only Loans

Ideal if you're an independent contractor who gets paid on 1099 and can document consistent deposits.

## DSCR Loans (for investors)

If you're buying a rental property, lenders can approve you based on the property's cash flow — not your personal income.

(These feel like magic, but they're just smart math.)

These programs usually come with slightly higher rates or down payments, but they offer freedom that traditional mortgages don't.

## How to Prepare Like a Pro

Here are the most important "smooth, no-stress" steps:

Make sure your past 12–24 months of income tell a stable story.

Have your business bank statements clean and easy to read.

Know what you wrote off — and whether those deductions help or hurt your mortgage goals.

Give your lender a complete picture instead of separate puzzle pieces.

The goal is not perfection.

It's clarity.

.   .   .

## The Mindset Shift

Being self-employed doesn't make you a complicated borrower.

It makes you a creative one.

You built your income your way — and lenders simply need to understand it.

With the right preparation and the right loan program, you can buy a home confidently, proudly, and without feeling like your entrepreneurship is a problem to solve.

It's not a problem.

It's your superpower.

You just needed the guidebook — and look at that... you have it now.

\* \* \*

# ⭐ CHAPTER 19

## THE LAST PAGE — AND THE NEXT BEGINNING

You made it to the final chapter — which means you're not just informed…

you're *dangerously* informed.

(in the very best way)

At this point, you understand the mortgage world better than most people who work in it — and now it's time to translate that knowledge into real life. This chapter gathers the most helpful tools, websites, and moments when you'll want to come back and reread certain parts of this book. No fluff. No overwhelm. Just clarity and support, exactly when you need it.

## Tools That Actually Make Home buying Easier

There are a million apps and calculators out there, but these are the ones worth your time — the ones that help you prepare instead of confuse you.

### A solid budget calculator

Not the kind that makes you feel guilty — the kind that helps you understand what you can *comfortably* afford without sacrificing your sanity or your brunch plans.

### A reliable mortgage calculator

Something simple that estimates payments, taxes, insurance, and the real monthly number you'll see when everything is said and done. Not glamorous, but extremely helpful.

### A credit-monitoring app

Credit Karma, Experian, PrivacyGuard — any tool that helps you stay aware of your score and keeps you from being surprised during pre-approval.

### A clean document checklist

Because the fastest way to get a smooth pre-approval is having your documents ready before anyone asks.

### A moving checklist

Moving is organized chaos. A checklist keeps at least some of it under control — boxes included.

### Websites Worth Bookmarking

Think of these as your "adulting but smarter" resources:

• **HUD.gov** — grants, down payment assistance, FHA information

• **CFPB.gov** — trustworthy financial tools and explanations

• **Your local county website** — property taxes, homestead exemption, local rules

• **Zillow / Redfin / Realtor.com** — for browsing, researching, and daydreaming

These sites are for information — not for choosing your lender.

You already have a Lily for that. 😉

## When to Revisit This Book

This book isn't a one-time read.

It's a resource — one you'll come back to whenever life shifts and your mortgage world needs a tune-up.

Come back to it when you're:

• thinking about refinancing

• getting a raise or changing jobs

• exploring investment properties

• wanting to remove mortgage insurance

- needing a quick numbers refresher

- feeling confused about your next step

The answers won't change — but *you* will grow into them differently each time.

## Your Next Chapter (Yes — You Definitely Have One)

Whether you're buying your first home, upgrading, downsizing, investing, refinancing, or planning an entirely new chapter, you are no longer guessing. You understand this process with clarity and confidence — the kind most people never get.

You've built a mindset that combines knowledge, stability, and intention.

And when you approach homeownership this way, you don't just buy a property…

you build a life.

A foundation.

A future with options.

Your home is not the finish line — it's the beginning of generational stability, financial growth, and a life you get to design on purpose.

And this book?

It's just the starting point.

I'm cheering you on — always. 🩶

\* \* \*

# 📖 GLOSSARY
## MAKING MORTGAGE LANGUAGE HUMAN

Most mortgage glossaries read like they were written by a very tired attorney. Not this one. This glossary is your *"explain it to me like I'm a real person"* guide. No stiff definitions, no confusing jargon — just clear language you can actually use.

Use this chapter whenever you run into a mortgage term that makes you pause and say, "Wait... what?"

Here we go — clean, simple, human definitions:

### Adjustable-Rate Mortgage (ARM)

A loan with an interest rate that can change after an initial fixed period. Starts lower, adjusts later.

.   .   .

## Amortization

How your mortgage is paid down over time through principal and interest.

## Amortization Schedule

A full breakdown of every payment you'll make until the loan is paid off.

## Annual Percentage Rate (APR)

Your interest rate plus certain lender fees, shown as one combined percentage.

## Application Fee

A fee some lenders charge to begin processing your loan.

## Appraisal

A professional estimate of your home's value.

## Appraisal Gap

The difference between the agreed purchase price and the appraised value.

· · ·

## Assets

Cash or valuables you own that help demonstrate financial stability.

## Basis Points (bps)

Small rate movements. One hundred basis points equal one percent.

## Bank Statement Loan

A loan that uses bank statements instead of tax returns to calculate income.

## Bridge Loan

Short-term financing used to buy a new home before selling your current one.

## Cash to Close

The total amount you need to bring to closing, including down payment and closing costs.

## Closing Disclosure (CD)

A five-page document showing your final loan terms, fees, and monthly payment.

## Clear to Close (CTC)

The final approval from underwriting confirming that you're ready for closing.

## Closing Costs

The fees required to finalize a mortgage, such as taxes, insurance, lender, and title fees.

## Co-Borrower

Someone who applies for the loan with you to help you qualify.

## Collections

Past due debts reported on your credit. Best handled with guidance from your lender.

## Concessions

Money the seller agrees to contribute toward your closing costs.

. . .

## Conforming Loan

A loan that meets Fannie Mae and Freddie Mac requirements.

## Conventional Loan

A traditional mortgage not backed by federal programs.

## Credit Inquiry – Hard Pull

A full credit check that may temporarily affect your score.

## Credit Inquiry – Soft Pull

A credit check that does not affect your score.

## Credit Score

A number that reflects your credit history, typically ranging from 300 to 850.

## Debt-to-Income Ratio (DTI)

The percentage of your income that goes toward monthly debt obligations.

. . .

## Deed

The legal document proving homeownership.

## Default

Failure to make mortgage payments as agreed.

## Discount Points

Upfront payments made to lower your interest rate.

## Down Payment

The amount of money you pay upfront toward the purchase price of a home.

## Earnest Money Deposit (EMD)

A deposit given to show serious intent when making an offer on a home.

## Equity

Your home's value minus the amount you still owe.

. . .

## Escrow Account

An account holding funds for property taxes and insurance.

## Escrow Shortage

When your escrow account does not contain enough money due to tax or insurance increases.

## FHA Loan

### *(Federal Housing Administration)*

A government-backed loan with flexible qualifications and a minimum 3.5% down payment.

## First-Time Homebuyer

Anyone who has not owned a home in the past three years.

## Fixed-Rate Mortgage

A mortgage with an interest rate that remains the same for the life of the loan.

## Gift Funds

Financial gifts from family or approved donors used toward your down payment or closing costs.

## Hazard Insurance

Another name for homeowners insurance.

## HELOC

Home Equity Line of Credit secured by your home's equity.

## Home Inspection

A professional evaluation of a home's condition before purchase.

## Homeowners Association (HOA)

A governing body that manages shared areas, rules, and community standards.

## Homestead Exemption

A property tax reduction for primary residences.

## Interest Rate

The cost of borrowing money, expressed as a percentage.

## Loan Estimate (LE)

A document showing estimated loan terms, costs, and monthly payments, provided early in the process.

## Loan Officer

Your mortgage professional who guides you through the process.

## Loan Servicer

The company you make your mortgage payments to.

## Loan-to-Value Ratio (LTV)

The percentage of the home's value that is financed.

## MIP

Mortgage Insurance Premium associated with FHA loans.

## Mortgage Insurance (PMI)

Insurance added to some loans when the down payment is less than twenty percent.

## Origination Fee

A lender fee for processing your loan application.

## P&I

The principal and interest portion of your monthly payment.

## PITI

Principal, interest, taxes, and insurance combined into your total monthly payment.

## Rate Lock

A guarantee that your interest rate will not change for a specified period.

## Recasting

Reducing your monthly payment by applying a lump sum toward principal without refinancing.

. . .

## Recording Fee

The fee paid to officially register your property purchase with the county.

## Reserves

Additional funds required by lenders to demonstrate financial stability after closing.

## Revolving Debt

Debt such as credit cards or lines of credit that can vary each month.

## Settlement Agent

The professional or title company managing closing documents and funds.

## Short Sale

A sale where the home is sold for less than the amount owed on the mortgage.

## Survey

A map showing your property's boundaries and structures.

. . .

## Term

The length of your mortgage, such as fifteen or thirty years.

## Title Insurance

Protection against ownership disputes or past property issues.

## Underwriting

The detailed review of your financial documents for loan approval.

## USDA

## United States Department of Agriculture Loan

A government-backed mortgage program that offers **0%** down payment for homes in eligible rural and suburban areas.

## Verification of Employment (VOE)

The lender's confirmation that you are currently employed.

. . .

## Verification of Rent (VOR)

Documentation showing timely rent payments.

## VA

## Department of Veterans Affairs Loan

A powerful loan program for veterans, active-duty service members, and eligible surviving spouses.

* * *

# MINI INVESTOR GLOSSARY

**After Repair Value (ARV)**

The estimated value of a property after renovations.

**Cap Rate**

A measure of return based on net operating income divided by purchase price.

**Cash-on-Cash Return**

The annual cash flow divided by the amount of cash invested.

**Depreciation**

A tax benefit allowing you to deduct the property's wear and tear.

## DSCR

Debt Service Coverage Ratio—rental income divided by mortgage payment.

## Net Operating Income (NOI)

Income after expenses, not including the mortgage payment.

## Vacancy Rate

The percentage of time a rental property is expected to be unoccupied.

\* \* \*

# SELF-EMPLOYED GLOSSARY

## 1099 Income

Compensation received as an independent contractor.

## Profit and Loss Statement (P&L)

A document summarizing business income and expenses.

## Business Deposits

Deposits used to verify income for bank-statement loans.

## Expense Factor

A percentage lenders apply to estimate business expenses.

LILY DOMINGUEZ

* * *

# CLOSING DAY GLOSSARY

## Final Walkthrough

Your last check of the home before closing.

## Funding

When your lender releases the loan money.

## Signing Appointment

The meeting where you sign the final paperwork.

## Recording

The moment the county officially registers you as the homeowner.

LILY DOMINGUEZ

* * *

# ♥ A FINAL NOTE FROM LILY

If you're reading this last page, pause and appreciate what you just accomplished. You didn't just finish a mortgage book — you showed up for yourself. You chose to learn something most people avoid because it feels "too hard" or "too confusing." You took the time to understand money, mindset, and homeownership in a way that will support you for years to come.

Whether this book helped you take your first step or your fifteenth, I'm truly honored to be part of your journey. Helping people find confidence, clarity, and peace around the mortgage process is one of my greatest joys — and you are the reason why.

And if you ever need guidance, encouragement, or simply someone to explain things like a real human again... I'm here. Always cheering you on and always rooting for you.

Your dream, your home, your future — you've got this.

With so much love and pride,

**Lily** ♥

* * *

## THE MORTGAGE MATH

This is the book where mortgage math stops being scary

and starts being your new party trick.

Payments? Easy.

Interest? Light work.

Rental math? A joke.

PMI? Please.

**These numbers are about to behave so nicely, you'll
think they're flirting.**

If *The Mortgage Mindset* made you confident,

*The Mortgage Math* is going to make you unstoppable —

and maybe even a little insufferable at brunch

(but in a very, very impressive way). 🖤🔲😎🔥

# ABOUT THE AUTHOR

**Lily Dominguez** is a bilingual Mortgage Loan Originator, real estate investor, educator, and lifelong student of wealth-building through homeownership. For more than 25 years, Lily has not only helped others navigate the mortgage world — she's lived it herself, building her own real estate portfolio one property, one lesson, and one strategy at a time.

Today, Lily is known for her warm, judgment-free approach and her uncanny ability to explain complex mortgage concepts in plain, human language. She is also the creator of **The Speaks Human System™**, a communication framework designed to simplify the mortgage process through clarity, empathy, and confidence — the same approach woven throughout this book. Her clients often say she makes them feel safe, supported, and understood.

She specializes in first-time homebuyers, self-employed borrowers, and real estate investors. Whether she's breaking down DSCR loans, guiding someone through their first pre-approval, or helping a family move into their dream home, Lily brings the same blend of professionalism, empathy, and "okay, let's make this simple" energy to every conversation.

When she's not guiding clients to closing day, you'll find her on the tennis court working on her backhands and forehands, in her kitchen experimenting with hazelnut chocolate gelato, wild-mushroom risotto, or delicate apple roses, relaxing at the beach, or exploring new cities.

She lives in Florida and continues to serve homebuyers, investors, and dreamers — one conversation, one mindset shift, and one mortgage at a time.

* * *

www.ingramcontent.com/pod-product-compliance
Lightning Source LLC
Chambersburg PA
CBHW030523210326
41597CB00013B/1004